Scary Stories to Tell to Millennials

Scary Stories to Tell to Millennials

A Humorous and Unsettling Collection of Post-Modern Horror Stories

J. R. Salem

Table of Contents

Foreword

Wandering through a B. Dalton Bookseller in the early 1990's, my third-grade self happened upon a thin, black book sitting on a shelf display. A closer inspection of the cover caused me to be taken aback: the stark, black-and-white charcoal image of a grinning skull stared directly into me. I was instantly overcome with curiosity. Grabbing the book off the display, I flipped through it, taking in more unsettling artwork and skimming some of the large-print horror stories and urban legends. I was never the same after my encounter with Alvin Schwartz' *Scary Stories to Tell in the Dark*, and the illustrations by Stephen Gammell intrigue me to this day. To that end, I felt it necessary to conjure my own tales of horror, reframed for middle age and the trials that are facing many of us today. I hope this work brings you an

1

ounce of the mystery and wonder I felt as a kid, and that you find some humor in the following tales. These are crafted to reflect the new, digital frontier that has been laid out before us. Accompanying each story is an illustration generated by artificial intelligence, somehow fitting for this collection of tales. Enjoy, and beware.

-   J. R. Salem

The Housing Market

John and Makenzie sat in their dimly-lit, basement studio efficiency apartment. The drip-drip-drip of the leaky shower and the rattling of the metal grate on their window added a soundtrack to their nightly endeavor: searching for a house. The owner of the crumbling three-story building in which they lived had decided to sell the property, and John and Makenzie had been served a 60-day eviction notice. They were getting desperate.

Their nightly search, huddled under blankets on their sofa to ward out the early spring chill, was routine by now. Their sunken eyes, deepened by sleepless nights awash in the anxiety of impending homelessness, pored endlessly over internet real estate listings.

Both John and Makenzie had gone to college, gotten decent jobs, and managed to save a modest sum for a down payment. However, just as their dream of home ownership appeared within grasp, a dark specter settled across the land, chilling their dreams. It was referred to around office spaces, grocery stores, and quiet dinner tables as The Housing Market.

Prices for properties soared, and those desperate for refuge from housing impermanence fled to the ever-dwindling rental market, driving rents upward. With little hope, the couple continued their fruitless hunt. Until one click landed them on something unbelievable.

Before their eyes was a listing with a single picture. 24 Edgewood Drive. The image showed a modest Cape Cod style home, with a generous yard, a neat wooden fence, a brick walkway, and a crooked wooden treehouse. The listing stated, "Priced to move! Motivated seller, no showing, property as-is. All offers entertained."

The couple was suspicious, but the price seemed too good to be true. Of course, maybe this was a fixer-upper, or something was amiss, but even still, the price was unbelievable. The couple checked a few other real estate sites, and found the exact listing: a single image, the same description, and the same price. After a brief consultation, the couple quickly fired off an email to the seller's agent: "When can we view the property?"

The night passed slowly, as the couple attempted to sleep, feeling the desperation only those imminently homeless have. Thoughts raced through their minds as they dared dream of a refuge from their dripping, rattling, musty, basement studio. At three a.m., John's phone buzzed on the plastic storage bin he used as a nightstand. Makenzie shifted, tensed, and nudged John. His heart was racing as he reached over, the bright glow of the small screen burning his eyes.

As the blindness subsided, he saw he had a new email: "No showings, bids accepted until midnight tomorrow. Please make an offer. Serious buyers only." He gasped and prodded Makenzie, who rolled over and rubbed her eyes. She read the text

5

and replied, "Make the offer." He quickly thumbed a response, giving their best price. It would be an expensive mortgage for the two of them, even with their down payment. He sighed, and prepared for the rejection that inevitably came.

The next day, the couple tiredly shuffled off to work, the business of the house getting lost in the mess of their office jobs and the thousand other little trials. When they met at the paint-chipped door of their basement studio that evening and John had not heard any response, they decided to go for a drive past 24 Edgewood Drive.

The couple climbed into John's old Honda, and through the mist of the early spring evening, they made their way to the other side of town that housed Edgewood. As they drove, they began passing small shops. Then bigger shops, bigger houses, manicured lawns, trimmed hedges, and even gated homes. As they approached Edgewood, Makenzie began feeling the faint stirring of optimism. She began to imagine a life in this world, of brunch at the corner cafe and quick trips to the organic grocery store in the neighborhood. As they inched closer to Edgewood,

John began imagining playing with future children in the expansive front yards, and of smoky back patio cookouts with laughing friends in golf polos. Out of the cloud of hope, the Cape Cod from the listing drifted into view.

The home looked perfect. It had a beautiful lawn, clean siding, and a new-looking roof. It looked just like the picture. They pulled the car over, got out, and gingerly approached the door. They knocked, hoping to catch a glimpse of the interior, but were unanswered. The curtains were drawn, and there was no way to view inside. However, to the couple, it didn't matter at this point: they were sold.

Another sleepless night rolled by, the drip-drip-drip of the leaky shower and the rattling of the window bars seemed to intensify, calling to John and Makenzie as if the old studio was beckoning for them to stay. The darkness crept on, washing the couple in a timeless void. Until, again, at three in the morning, the plastic storage bin rattled John awake. His heart leapt in his chest.

"Offer Accepted," was all the email said. His breath caught in his throat as he stifled a gleeful cry. Makenzie shot awake, glaring at John. He showed her the bright screen, and rubbing away the sleep, her face exploded in a gleeful smile as she realized what the message said. They were to be homeowners.

The next day, correspondence moved quickly between the couple and the realtor. Paperwork was sent back and forth electronically, with requests to electronically sign, receive loan documents, and view tax certificates. The couple conferred via hushed phone calls, attempting to quickly resolve the matters at hand so they could move on to the exciting business of imagining their newfound life.

They were assured by the realtor that everything was in order, that the home was in perfect condition, and that the reason there was no showing was that the owner had passed and the heirs were from out of town and could not be bothered with accommodating any potential buyers. This was, after all, customary under the conditions of the Housing Market.

Days and then weeks passed as the couple packed their belongings into John's old Honda, ahead of their impending eviction. Their closing date was a day after they had to be out of their dripping, rattling, musty, decrepit old basement studio. They spent that night in the car.

The next day, the couple pulled up in front of 24 Edgewood Drive. Despite their rough night in the car, John and Makenzie jumped out of their seats when a new-looking foreign-made SUV pulled up. Out stepped a neatly-dressed blonde woman in an expensive-looking pantsuit. She looked around casually, until her eyes landed on the weary couple, then her face exploded with a practice smile that nonetheless eased John and Makenzie at once.

The woman strode over to them, standing in front of the neat little fence. She shook their hands and presented them with the key. "Congratulations," she said, "You made a very competitive offer and I'm sure you are thrilled. Let me show you around."

John and Makenzie grasped the key, and ran to the front door, only to find that there must be something wrong with the lock. Or the key.

"No, sillies!" The woman yelled, as she made her way down the neat brick path to the back yard. The couple, confused, followed her. "Up there!" She laughed, pointing to a thick tree, near a dangling rope ladder. The couple, bewildered, eyed the ramshackle, crooked treehouse. At the base of the tree was a neat little sign that read, "24 Edgewood Drive." The realtor patted the trunk and said, "That's the Housing Market for you."

Brayden, Hunter, Riley

Kevin Dillon finally got a few days off from work. He had been putting in 50 hours plus at his office job, and decided to use some of his PTO to get away for a bit. He found himself on the edge of a small lake, enjoying the sun, sand, and calm water. He intended to shut off all electronics, and he didn't even bring his work laptop. His boss could figure it all out while he's off. Or so he hoped.

Kevin sat back in his beach chair, closed his eyes, and let his mind wander. He tuned into the sounds around him: the distant whoosh of cars passing the nearby mountain road, the giggles of children playing near the shore, the hum of small boat engines at the far end of the lake, a far-off Bluetooth speaker softly bleating country rock. Paradise, Kevin thought. He tuned in to the sounds, letting the sun wash over his face, and he began to drift off.

BRAYDEN. HUNTER. RILEY. The words hit him like a semi-truck, nearly knocking him out of his seat. BRAYDEN. HUNTER. RILEY. Again, the staccato blasted him alert, like he was taking fire from a machine-gun. His eyes snapped open to see a heavily tattooed woman in a tankini standing knee-deep in the lake water, three children under the age of nine, he guessed, splashing happily by her feet. BRAYDEN. HUNTER. RILEY. She crowed again. Clearly unhappy with what the kids were doing, or attempting to get their attention, she continued to call their names as though the children were lost down a well.

Kevin sat back, attempting to ignore this intrusion into his peace. He closed his eyes again, trying to listen to the tune playing distantly on the speaker, or the passing cars. BRAYDEN. HUNTER. RILEY. The voice, each time, becoming more grating to his ears. The names began running together in his mind, no longer sounding like names but more like an incantation.

13

He had finally had enough. He got out of his chair and went over to the woman, wading out into the lake water. "Hey, people are trying to relax here, do you think you can keep it down?" He said. The woman rounded on him, and the look in her eyes told him instantly he had made a gross miscalculation. She opened her mouth, and like the horn of an ancient mountain shepherd, she trumpeted, BRAYDEN. HUNTER. RILEY. LET'S GO! WE'RE LEAVING!

Kevin locked eyes with the woman, whose smoldering gaze burned something deep into his soul. She whispered to him as she rushed past, three children's arms and legs somehow all tangled in hers, "If I can't have any peace, neither can you." She then stormed away, a tangle of wet bathing suits, lake water, and the cacophony that accompanied them.

Later that night, Kevin returned to his rented lake house, a case of beer and a couple steaks in tow. He grilled, drank and forgot all about the woman at the lake. He drifted off to a dreamless slumber, cares washed away by the water, sun, and light beer.

BRAYDEN. HUNTER. RILEY. It struck him like lightning, and he jolted upright in bed. He stopped to listen in the absolute quiet, and then his ears were met with silence. He began to laugh to himself. The lady's constant screeching from earlier had worked its way into his dreams! He chuckled some more, thought about the nightmare it must be minding after three kids, and went back to sleep.

BRAYDEN.HUNTER.RILEY. Again, like a sonic boom, this time somehow louder. He knew he didn't dream it this time. He got out of bed and wandered around the lake house, not sure what he was looking for, or what he would find. Tired, and satisfied no one was there to play a prank on him, he returned to bed.

BRAYDEN. HUNTER. RILEY burst into his ears. This time, he was wide awake. Then he heard it again. And again. Six times that night, like someone shouting two inches from his ears, he heard it. BRAYDEN. HUNTER. RILEY.

He returned home the next day, sleepless. He then went back to work. He tried to function, but he couldn't concentrate. At unpredictable intervals, he heard the scream. BRAYDEN. HUNTER. RILEY. It slowly drove him crazy, he began shouting it out at work. His boss, concerned for his mental health, was initially sympathetic.

After months, Kevin was unemployed, and a hermit in his own home. He tried to track the woman down, but it was useless. He had no idea where she came from, where she lived, or who she was. He tried googling the kids' names, but the number of people with Braydens, Hunters, and Rileys was immense.

One day, at the grocery store, he had a particularly bad episode. BRAYDEN. HUNTER. RILEY. The words exploded in his brain, over and over again, until the names became meaningless syllables crowding out all other senses and thought. He collapsed on the floor, and everything faded to black.

Kevin woke up, strapped to a gurney. A medical attendant came along his side, and said, "Sounds like you had quite the episode. We'll get you some medicine to help you feel better, but

17

it looks like you'll be with us for a little while. I'll just go get the doctor."

The attendant stepped into the hall, and closed the door behind her until only a sliver of light poured in. Kevin heard the attendant murmur something, and the attendant was replaced by a dark figure in the doorway. A woman in a white, short-sleeved lab coat and surgical mask stepped into the room. As she drew closer, he recognized a tattoo on one of her forearms.

"I told you, if I don't get any peace, neither will you," the woman said, slipping down her mask to reveal a face that had haunted him since that day at the lake. She produced a long syringe and jabbed it into his arm. As he felt his eyes grow heavy and the light dim around him, he caught a glimpse of the woman's name tag, and he was sure, at that moment, that he had been driven mad. The tag read: Dr. Brayden Hunter-Riley.

The Subscription Box

Julianne was bored at work one day, sitting in her half-cubicle, attempting to look busy. She was really skimming through her social media feed on her smartphone, surreptitiously half-covered with a legal notepad on her desk. Browsing was frowned upon during work hours. Her index finger glided slowly over the surface, advancing the little boxes filled with pictures and text, spinning upward like a small, glowing slot machine.

Her finger paused for a brief second as a dark picture slid into view. An advertisement confronted her with the image of an old, worn-looking cardboard box sitting on a desk in an office that could have been from 1992. The box perched on a scratched wooden desk, and in the background, a large tan monitor sat on a squat, matching computer. A worn, gray fabric roller chair with yellow foam peeking from the top edge sat forlornly at the edge of the picture.

Amidst the endless high-rise glamour shots and white sandy beaches usually careening across her little screen, this image was out of place. *Ugly,* she thought, but something about the advertisement drew her in.

Are you looking for excitement? Do you wish mysteries were awaiting you? Look no further, the ad promised. Despite her better judgement, she clicked the ad. It opened a website with flashing text and flames, on a bright blue background. She hadn't seen a site designed like this in forever, and it made her smile a little.

THE FAMOUS MYSTERY BOX. The text flashed, and she scrolled for more. The site promised to deliver one box full of mysteries beyond your wildest dreams every month. She had heard of these subscription boxes, where companies hand-select interesting items and mail them out to people looking for a little variety. She had never ordered one of these services, but she was definitely looking for a little variety in her life. She looked up to see the cubicle farm extending into eternity around her, a study in Griege.

She returned to the little glowing screen below her, promising to spice up her life a little bit. The site guaranteed limited edition, curated products from all corners of the earth, specially selected by the company's buyers. Even better, the first box was free if she committed to six months. Before she could reconsider, she tapped in her credit card information and the order was sent.

A rush filled Julianne, welling up from her knees and rising through her body, flushing her face. Was this excitement? She felt like a kid awaiting a wished-for gift on Christmas Eve. She grinned to herself, staring at the little order confirmation screen, when she was startled by the disapproving eyes of her boss wandering through the area. She quickly flipped over her phone, made an apologetic face toward her boss, and returned to work.

Julianne, in fact, forgot she had placed this order at all. That is, until four days later, when she stumbled up her concrete steps to find an ugly, brown box sitting on her porch. It dawned on her that this must be her first shipment, but the box looked like it had been kicked down a flight of stairs. She nevertheless scooped it up and hurried inside.

Julianne sat the box down on her coffee table and got to work removing the yellowed paper tape holding the lid shut. *This must be part of the gimmick,* she thought. Upon opening the box, a musty aroma hit her, along with a cloud of dust. Moving some crumpled brown craft paper out of the way, she observed an assortment of shapes wrapped in tissue paper.

Grabbing the first one excitedly, she tore into the paper to find a statue of an elephant carved out of what appeared to be jade. It looked beautiful. The next parcel held a heavy bracelet, with what appeared to be real jewels, set in gold. Was this real? She was enamored.

Five little presents later, she beheld the final tissue-wrapped object. She eagerly unwrapped it to find a jeweled skull. Very interesting, but not really her style. She gathered up her items with glee and set about her apartment to display her new treasures. She could not wait for the next box.

Later that night, Julianne was awoken by a sound in her empty apartment. It seemed to be coming from the living room. It sounded like soft crying. She got out of bed and crept to the bedroom door. She opened it, only to find the noises continued from behind her couch. As she got closer, the noises stopped. Sitting on the ground, behind the couch, was the jade elephant.

Julianne decided the next day to take her newfound trinkets to a local gold and jewelry shop that specialized in antiques. Inside, the owner confirmed that the bracelet was indeed real gold, and had real rubies. He also told her, to her dismay, that the jeweled skull looked like it might be real, and he was not sure it was legal for her to even own it. She decided to sell the skull and the elephant, along with a few other things, but kept the bracelet. She earned enough to treat herself and a couple friends to a nice dinner at her favorite Dim Sum restaurant with plenty to spare. Her friends all commented on how much they loved her new bracelet.

Concerns over the contents of the surprise box were salved by the tidy sum she earned from disposing of some of the more questionable items, and while not everything was her taste, she felt a tinge of danger and excitement. She quickly forgot about the crying elephant.

Weeks later, another box appeared. Somewhat less enthusiastically than last time, she carried the battered box inside and set it down. This time, she didn't look at it right away. However, her curiosity got the better of her, and later that evening she tore into it.

Inside, she found more items wrapped in tissue paper. These items were much less alluring, and seemed like somebody's cast-off junk. She wondered if the curators were simply selling off things they found in storage unit auctions. That idea satisfied her as she dug through the box of old floppy disks, a creepy doll with a square wooden head, four packs of unopened baseball cards, and a Lucite cube with what looked like a human tooth inside.

That night, she was again awoken by what sounded like a group of people murmuring in her living room. Terrified, she called the police, only to find that no one was in the room. The cop seemed less than pleased, but was friendly enough. The next day, she went to take the box to the trash when a neighbor eyed the packs of baseball cards and offered her fifty bucks. She accepted.

For weeks, Julianne was awoken early in the morning by loud noises, whispers, footsteps, and other strange sounds. She found her cupboards open and things strewn around her apartment when she got home from work. One day, her refrigerator was opened, spoiling all the food inside. She was not sure what to do about these things, but she wouldn't have to worry long.

As another month rolled around, she returned home to a sight that now sickened her: a dirty, wrinkled cardboard box. She did not even take it inside this time, she tore it apart on her stoop to find tissue paper-wrapped animal bones, jars filled with green and brown liquid that contained pieces of something floating in the murk, and something that made her stomach drop. At the bottom of the box was a wallet, with the driver's license of a Benjamin Doone, and a thousand dollars cash in hundred dollar bills. Horrified, she threw everything in the trash except the wallet.

Days later, Julianne was visited at work by the police. They asked to speak to her in private. They all stepped outside, and she was told that she was the subject of an ongoing investigation and they needed her to come make a statement. She was floored. She inquired about what crime they think she committed, but they firmly recommended she come speak with them. Panicked, knowing she had a man's wallet in her purse, she asked if she could come down tomorrow.

The police agreed, but stated that the matter was very serious, and they thought she had some information about missing persons. They said she had sold some things to a pawn shop a couple months ago they needed to talk to her about. Julianne returned home that evening in a panic. She wasn't sure what to do with Mr. Doone's wallet, she hadn't slept in weeks, and she was in fear of being arrested for a crime.

Awaiting her was another box. Only one day later. She screamed a guttural animal scream and ripped the top flaps off. Inside, she saw a single, folded piece of notebook paper. She unfolded the paper to see, in typewriter print:

FOR CANCELLATIONS PLEASE APPEAR IN PERSON AT 1140 MARSH STREET UNIT 14. CANCELLATIONS MUST BE MADE IN PERSON AND MUST BE WITHIN 24 HOURS OF THE RECEIPT OF THIS NOTICE.

That evening, desperate, and in fear of being arrested by the police, Julianne drove to the location on the note. Putting aside all of her reservations, she was simply desperate to put the whole matter to rest. She hoped what she would find was that her situation was all a misunderstanding and she could confidently go to the police tomorrow and settle the whole matter. She strode up to the dark, industrial building and knocked on the door of 1140 Marsh Street, Unit 14.

The next day, Julianne's office stood empty. No one noticed. Her half-cubicle sat silent while the other office inhabitants quietly and dully went about their business. Business as usual was boring.

Many rows down, in a different section of the mid-rise building housing Julianne's slice of cubicle hell, a woman named Joan got an email sent from Julianne's work email. Joan clicked the email, and it brought up an advertisement promising an escape from boredom, one mystery subscription box at a time. Joan subscribed.

Days later, Joan came to work, a large smile on her face. On her wrist was a beautiful, golden bracelet filled with rubies.

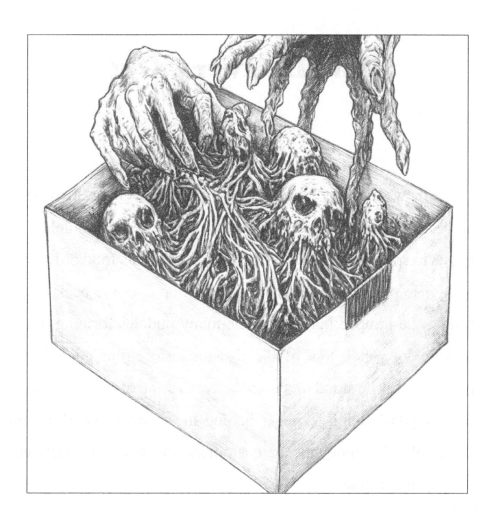

29

The Delivery Gig

Matthew sat in his car on a rainy summer evening, the ripped blades of his wipers squeaking across his cracked windshield. His phone beeped, and he looked down to see that his food order was ready. He pulled the collar of his jacket up over the back of his head as he jumped into one of the many puddles forming in the parking lot. The glow of the fast-food storefront guided him inside, and as he stood in the doorway, shaking off the rain water, an annoyed-looking teenager behind the counter glared at him from behind a long line of customers and pointed, "Delivery drivers in that line."

Matthew shuffled over to the line of bedraggled looking folks carrying insulated bags. As another worker called out names, the drivers hurriedly snatched up their orders and fled into the wet darkness. *Hurry up, I have two other orders waiting on me,* he thought. A name was called that matched Matthew's customer, and he loaded up and headed back on the road.

Stomping up the dark driveway, he was greeted at the door by a nice-looking blonde woman in sweats. He proffered up the wet plastic bag and did his best to muster a cheerful "Have a great night!"

She smirked at him, stated the food felt cold, rolled her eyes and slammed the door. His phone beeped that an order was completed. Three stars and a two-dollar tip. Matthew headed back out into the drizzle.

This was Matthew's second job, something he did in the evenings to make a few extra bucks. He was divorced, and making child support payments to his ex-wife meant that every penny mattered. Even on good nights like this, it meant an endless carousel of irritable restaurant employees and nonplussed couch potatoes too tired, lazy, unwilling or unable to collect their own takeout. The money was inconsistent, but he like the autonomy. When he had his kids, he wasn't tied to begging a boss at a part-time job for the nights off.

Driving on to the next stop, he thought, *there's gotta be a better way.* He wondered if going to a nicer part of town, delivering groceries, or doing rideshares would be more lucrative. As it stood, he thought he might even be losing money this month, as tips weren't as generous as usual.

At the next stop, he ran into a guy waiting for an order, but he didn't recognize the logo on the green cooler he carried. Matthew asked the man, and the guy said it was a new delivery app. He said that it wasn't popular in the area yet, but it paid much better than the big names. He warned Matthew not to cut into his turf, but Matthew was usually working the other side of town. The guy encouraged him to download the app and try it out.

The next day, Matthew rolled out of bed, late for work, and made his way into the coffee shop he called his day job. Later, on a break, he looked up the app, and downloaded it. On his way home, he got an alert: there was an order awaiting delivery, and the pay was twice what he would have gotten on his other gig. He didn't even think twice, and took the job.

He stopped off at a small deli in a part of his town he didn't usually frequent, went inside, and grabbed an order. It was pre-packaged in the bright green cooler he saw the other guy carrying. He took the food to the address, and was met at the door by the customer.

The man answered the door, wearing a pair of dirty jeans and a white T-shirt. The man was very pale, thin, and had piercing blue eyes. Matthew handed over the cooler, and the customer slurred, "Thankshh."

The customer disappeared inside only for a moment, returning with the empty cooler and two, crumpled, one-hundred dollar bills. "Hey, thanks yourself," Matthew said. He smiled to himself, thinking maybe things would work out after all. He kept an eye on the app the rest of the night. To his surprise and somewhat dismay, no other orders came in.

The next three days Matthew had his kids, so he couldn't take any jobs. About the same time every evening, an order would come in, and eventually a driver would take it. Few people used the app to order, though, it seemed.

A few days later, he returned to taking deliveries from the app. On his way home from work at the coffee shop, the familiar order would come in, he would pick it up, and he would be rewarded with a handsome cash tip upon delivery. He definitely could get used to this. One thing he noticed was that there seemed to be three or four different customers at the same house, and they all looked pale, almost sick. He figured they might be drug dealers or meth-heads, and in his mind, that was none of his business.

Day after day, he followed this routine, making enough money to fix up his old car, pay his ex-wife some extra for the kids' school clothes, and even buy a new couch for his apartment.

He kept taking the orders, a sense of comfort and routine settling in. However, he did notice the customers started looking sicker and sicker. He wondered if he should be worried. Was he running drugs? He never looked in the cooler, and it had not occurred to him until the thought that he might be a drug mule arose. He glanced in the back seat and noticed a transparent seal had been placed across the lid, making it evident if it was tampered-with.

Again, Matthew wasn't sure he cared. He wasn't doing anything wrong, he got an order through the app, picked it up at a deli, and delivered it. Hundreds of people in his city were ordering delivery food every week. Plus, the money was really good.

One dark and especially foggy night weeks later, Matthew dropped the food off, but the woman that answered the door looked different than the usual customer. In the dim light of his headlights, he though he saw bruises and cuts on her face and shoulders. Was she bleeding? He wasn't sure. Maybe she was being abused? He got concerned and asked her if she was okay. She just stared at him blankly, her jaw moving up and down, but no sound came out. He thought about calling the cops, but decided if there was drug activity, he didn't want to get caught up in it.

After he left, he felt guilty, and committed to ending his delivery streak to that residence. He worried it was dangerous, or there was something criminal happening there. As time went on, though, the other major delivery app got more competitive, and tips got fewer.

Against his better judgement, when the job came in one evening, he decided to take it. He was curious, after all, about the woman. Maybe he would find out that everything was fine. He picked up his familiar green cooler and headed over to the house.

When he arrived, he was greeted at the door by a relatively-healthy looking younger man, though still quite pale. The man grabbed the cooler, looked down, and furrowed his brow. Matthew noticed, then, that instead of a clear seal on the lid, there was a red seal. The man asked if he would step inside for a moment, and Matthew hesitated, but the man's smile disarmed

37

him, as well as a fist full of proffered cash.

Matthew stepped into the doorway, and immediately the door slammed behind him. Out of the darkness, he realized there were ten or fifteen people lying about the kitchen and living room. He didn't like this at all.

A cold hand grabbed his wrist, surprisingly strong. He looked up and it was a man with sores all over, missing an eye, and what appeared to be an exposed portion of his skull. Matthew looked down to see pieces of bone visible through ragged wounds on the man's hand. Matthew tried to scream but no sound came out.

The healthier-looking man popped open the cooler, and fished out a single human brain. He looked up at Matthew, a frown on his face.

"That's the problem with using this app," the man sighed. "When the product starts to run low, we end up having to eat the driver."

Do Not Disturb

Felicia stood at the wall of painted aluminum mailboxes in the hallway of her apartment building. The cheap indoor-outdoor carpet felt somehow damp beneath her socked feet, even though there was no rain or humidity in the air. She flipped the plain white envelope over in her hands a few times, examining her name and apartment number, hand-written on the front. The smell of cat litter and cigarettes hung in the hall, and she absently noticed the overhead light buzzing.

She knew what the envelope contained, her annual lease renewal. That meant rate increases. She had heard from some of her neighbors that this year, it wasn't pretty. She sighed.

As she returned to her apartment and slid the door closed, she tore into a corner with her fingernail and winced. A paper cut, great. Before the cut welled up with blood, she quickly tore open the envelope and took in the damage before the inevitable paper towel was needed to staunch the wound.

Her rent was going up nearly thirty percent. Thirty percent! She could barely afford the two-bedroom place she had now, especially after her ex-fiancé called everything off and moved out. With her nursing job, she was just making it now.

Felicia looked around her apartment, which she loved, but it was way too big for one person. There were one and a half bathrooms, a large common area, kitchen, balcony, and two big bedrooms. She decided maybe she needed a roommate.

That evening, Felicia sat hunched over her tablet and wrote up a listing on multiple apps and websites. She was very specific with her criteria: no men, no pets, and no noise during the day. The last was due to her shift at the hospital. After she finished posting, she looked up and huffed, letting herself deflate as she let out the breath she didn't realize she'd been holding. She liked living alone, but she'd be living in her car if she didn't get help.

A few days passed, and with her busy work schedule and some overtime shifts, she did not have time to check her messages on all the roommate sites. When she did, she had to wade through over a hundred messages from various creeps and sticklers. The handful of promising tenants either didn't respond or had found other arrangements by the time she got back in touch.

Felicia's leasing date grew closer, and she knew she could hold out a little while with some overtime and her savings, but she began to get somewhat desperate. She mentioned this to her mom on the phone, who was empathetic but otherwise unable to provide new ideas.

She was talking to another nurse one night, when he mentioned that in an online gaming chat he participated in, people regularly discuss looking for roommates or apartments. He said, half jokingly, that if anything came up, he'd pass it along to Felicia.

The next shift they worked together, the other nurse said, "You aren't going to believe this. I game with this girl who lives in a suburb nearby and she said she was looking to move out of her parent's house. I've played with her for a long time, she seems legit. I hope you don't mind, but I gave her your direct message account."

Felicia scoffed but didn't really mind. In fact, she was desperate enough to consider anyone at this point. She checked her messages and found that there was indeed a message from the gamer nickname that her coworker mentioned. She clicked open.

"Hi, this is Sophie, I heard you might be looking for a roommate. You can text me if your place is still available."

Felicia responded, and after a while of back-and-forth chatting, they agreed to meet up over the weekend. Sophie mentioned that she had severe anxiety and didn't really like to be out in public, so she would rather stop over to see the apartment. Felicia was initially reluctant, but after a video call, she felt a little more relaxed. Sophie seemed like a mild-mannered, sweet person. Felicia agreed to their visit.

On Saturday, Felicia awaited Sophie's visit, and invited a couple of friends over for a layer of safety. When Sophie arrived, everyone hit it off well, though Sophie was indeed shy. Sophie mentioned that she was not able to work due to anxiety and agoraphobia, and received a guaranteed government income, which she was desperate to get away from her greedy parents. She said that she mostly spent her time in her room playing video games, so she wouldn't be much of a presence in the apartment. She confided that it took everything she had to make the trek across town, but her anger over her parents' treatment of her condition was enough to overcome it. After a pleasant visit, Sophie agreed to the terms and said she would move in the following weekend. She paid Felicia a sizeable deposit, the total of what Sophie had been able to keep away from her mom and dad.

Sophie moved in, and to Felicia's pleasant surprise, the arrangement was better than she could have imagined. Sophie was a quiet housemate, and she liked to keep night hours, so they both slept during the day. Sophie's checks came like clockwork, and she stayed in her room many hours a day, busily gaming.

Sometimes, Felicia felt bad about Sophie being cooped up, and invited her to come out to the living room and watch TV or grab a coffee. Sophie would occasionally watch some TV with Felicia, but never took her up on her offer to leave the apartment. In fact, Felica often took care of groceries for them both, especially because it seemed that Sophie ate very little. Sophie was the perfect roommate.

After a while, Felica noticed that Sophie was not joining her for TV anymore, and she rarely was seen outside of her room. Felicia would knock on the door and check in on her, Sophie

responding that she was fine and would cheerfully wish Felicia a good night at work.

One day, Felica noticed a strange sign on the wall next to Sophie's room. The words looked like "Do Not Disturb" at first glance, but on inspection were oddly distorted. She continued to check on Sophie, but Sophie's responses were increasingly agitated. Further, Felica began hearing loud noises from the room, which she imagined were from whatever video game Sophie was playing.

Felicia also noticed that smaller amounts of food were being eaten day by day. One day, she knocked loudly on the door, asking Sophie to come out to talk to her. Felica was starting to get worried. Sophie angrily yelled through the door, "Leave me alone! I don't bother you all day!" Felicia called back that she really wanted her to come talk to her and Sophie screamed back to read the sign.

Felicia was getting annoyed, but decided she would respect her privacy. After all, she was paying, and she had the right to live her life how she wanted. At work, she shared her concerns with some coworkers, but nobody felt like there was anything Felicia could do if Sophie wasn't interested in communicating.

Felicia had several long nights of work in a row, even working a few back-to-back shifts requiring her to crash out on a couch in the nurse's lounge. Days had passed by the time she decided to check in with Sophie again.

This time, there was no response. Felicia knocked, but her knocks went unanswered. There were no game noises. The door was locked from the inside. Felicia decided Sophie must be sleeping and went about her business.

It was a while before the quiet broke her down. Felicia decided to force the door open, and what she found was beyond her worst fears.

Drawn on the floor was a series of unusual symbols, like something from astrology or an ancient language. In the center was a mummified body, dried as though it had been there for hundreds of years. On the still-lit screen was a page on an obscure

47

website detailing instruction for a magic spell to improve gaming performance. Jutting out of the mummy were bone-like spines, pointing in various directions toward the ceiling.

Felicia began to cry and thought about who she needed to call to get help. Then something cold gripped her heart, and she looked down at the pile of mail she had slid under the door. A new benefit check was there.

Felicia closed the door, grasped the check, and thought to herself, this is what Sophie would have wanted. She was the perfect roommate, after all.

Eternal Student Loans

Trevor wandered down the street, dejected. He went to the college of his dreams, only to be rejected from every job for which he had applied. Even worse, the first payment for his student loan was coming due next week. He needed a job, and fast.

After days of pounding the pavement, seeking applications at any place that was open, he finally took a job at a print shop in a rehabilitated old factory in a run-down area of the town. He felt a sense of relief, but hoped he could get a job in his chosen field, which was archaeology.

Time passed, and he worked hard at the print shop, even earning a small raise. He paid his bills as he could, but over time, he realized his student loans were getting larger the more he paid. After a year, panic began to set in as his student loan statement balance climbed higher and higher.

One day, on his walk home from work, he spotted a piece of paper nailed to a telephone pole. GOT STUDENT LOAN DEBT? WE CAN HELP. Trevor shook his head and continued past, figuring everyone must be finding themselves in this situation. He kept walking.

Weeks passed, and his daily walk past the ragged flyer continued to catch his curiosity. One day, after checking his bank account and finding exactly three dollars and twenty cents left until the next paycheck, he stopped and stared up at the flyer.

Well above his head, below the now-familiar words, was a QR code. He raised his phone, centered the code like a hunter sighting his prey, and snapped the link open. Nothing happened.

While at work, his phone dinged, and he checked it to see a text from an unknown number. The message read:

STUDENT LOANS PAID IN FULL. YOUR DEBT HAS BEEN CLEARED. AWAIT FURTHER NOTICE.

Trever laughed it off as one of the many spam messages sent daily. He went back to work, but later that evening he decided to log into his student loan account and check. To his surprise, the balance showed as zero, paid in full. He sat back, mouth agape. Did it really work? Was it that easy? He was sure there was a mistake, and when he checked tomorrow, the balance would be back to normal. Or higher.

Over the next several days Trevor checked, with a zero balance still being shown. He even got a congratulatory letter in the mail from the lender, indicating that his account was closed. One day, he tried logging in, only to find the account no longer was active.

Trevor used his savings from the student loan payments to buy a car, and he never passed by the old telephone pole again. He purchased a condo in a trendy area, one where live music played on Thursday nights and people went on wine walks. He loved it there.

A letter came in the mail for Trevor, and when he opened it, he was confused. It stated it was from the Archival Student Loan Repayment Program, and as a condition for full loan satisfaction, he was required to volunteer as listed. The only words below were: GO TO ST. MARK's CEMETERY AT DUSK. PLANT ONE MARIGOLD AT THE LISTED COORDINATES.

Trevor was creeped out but decided that it must be a religious organization that paid off his loans, and maybe this was the least he could do to repay their generosity. He stopped off at a garden center, picked up a pack of pre-potted marigolds, and drove to the cemetery. He used the GPS on his phone to find the coordinates, and after stumbling around in the dark he found an odd statue of a leprechaun, or at least a bearded man with a hat. He planted the flower, looked around to see if something meaningful happened, and then left.

A week or so later, another letter arrived. This one demanded he take a bottle of wine to a set of coordinates. This time, when he complied, he found himself outside an elementary school at 10:00 p.m.

Then another letter. And another. Soon, seemingly random tasks were piled upon him daily. Further, the tasks were getting stranger and stranger. They demanded he steal library books, then paint a face on the side of a building, then set a fire in a garbage can in the park. He decided that enough was enough and he would not comply any further. Every letter after, he threw promptly in the trash.

Days later, he received a notice that there had been an error with his student loans. His balance had been restored to its full amount, plus interest. He was despondent. With his new car and condo, there is no way he could pay the loan.

Another letter came from the Archival Student Loan Repayment Program, and again he threw it away. The next day, he got a letter from his condo leasing company that he had been deemed a credit risk and that they would need a security bond. Another letter came, and this time his car insurance went up, seemingly for no reason.

Finally, his boss called him into his office, and told Trevor that they had received an anonymous letter that he had been showing up to work drunk several days in a row, and demanded he obtain a substance abuse evaluation to keep his job.

Trevor got home that evening to find yet another letter from the Archival Student Loan Repayment Program. He opened it this time, only to find a folded piece of paper. Once opened, the paper revealed a single phrase, all in capitals, with a QR code underneath. GOT STUDENT LOAN DEBT? WE CAN HELP.

Trevor ran to a busy section of his neighborhood and stuck it on a sign board in the middle of a busy bar section. It was a nice night, and many people were out enjoying the bars and restaurants. He watched for a while from a park bench, but no one stopped at the sign.

He decided to get closer and found himself hiding in a bush near the signboard. An hour or so passed, and finally a dejected-looking woman stopped at the board, looked at the sign, and took out her phone. She held it up, and Trevor saw her flash activate.

Trevor woke up the next morning, checked his student loan account, and found that it was again a zero balance. He got a call from his boss that the letter seemed to all be a misunderstanding, and to forget all about it. Days passed, and his car insurance and condo were sorted out.

One evening, weeks later, Trevor was out to dinner with a girl he met in his building. The night was warm, and the company was perfect. Something yellow caught his eye, and he glanced over his shoulder to catch it. A familiar-looking woman was rushing down the sidewalk holding a potted marigold.

Gender Reveal Party

Rachel and Greg opened a brightly colored, oversized envelope. It was an invitation to their friends' Gender Reveal Party. Tiffany and Maxwell were expecting, and Tiffany was known for hosting extravagant events for the sake of social media clout. Greg groaned, knowing this event would be over the top. At least the food would be good. Rachel reminded him they had to get a gift. He groaned again.

The party was to be held at Tiffany's family cabin on the edge of her parents' expansive farm. "Tiffany's about to pop!" the invitation read, with images of Tiffany and Maxwell standing in a field of corn.

Greg and Rachel drove to the cabin, nestled on the edge of a vast cornfield in the middle of nowhere. There were cars lining the road, and a narrow dirt path stretched from the road to the cabin.

The party started cheerfully enough, but when the nature of the big reveal was learned, Greg got somewhat nervous. A huge box that looked like a popcorn container was wheeled into a clearing in the field, and everyone gathered around. Maxwell shouted that when he pressed a button, the box would pop open, releasing colored smoke and balloons. There appeared to be some kind of explosion that was about to happen during the reveal. Greg always felt that Tiffany was too dramatic.

As the crowd counted down from ten, Greg had a bad feeling. He looked over at Rachel, but she seemed caught up in the thrill of the reveal.

Three, two, one! The crowd shouted. Maxwell pushed the button, and a shockwave ripped through the crowd. Greg was knocked off his feet, and found himself staring up into the sky, his ears ringing.

He sat up, dazed and was enveloped in thick, black smoke. He called out for Rachel, and she cried out from somewhere in the haze. The smoke began to clear, and he saw the crowd stagger to their feet. Maxwell looked puzzled and ashamed, but Tiffany was oddly calm.

As the crowd came together, Greg suddenly felt dizzy, he looked around to see people coughing, vomiting blood, and as his vision dimmed, he thought he saw creatures dancing in the encroaching shadows. His eyes closed and he thudded to the ground.

When he awoke, it was pitch black, except for a faint orange glow at his feet. He tried to move, but realized he was tied to something. He looked around, and all the guests were in a circle in the field clearing, tied to wooden posts with their arms outstretched. His ankles were likewise bound to the base of the pole. His mouth was gagged, as he tried to scream out for Rachel.

The faint orange glow, he realized, was the beginning of a bonfire. The other guests began to scream as the fire crept up from below. Tiffany stepped into the center of the clearing.

Greg realized that Tiffany no longer appeared pregnant. Instead, cradled in her arms, was a hideous creature, and her face was covered in claw marks. The baby she was cradling looked like a goat with hook-like claws for hands.

"Sorry y'all, but the land gave me this baby, and now I need to feed the land. I hope you understand."

She set the tiny goat creature on the ground, and it set about tearing into each guest individually. Somehow, just as he felt his turn coming, he felt something sawing at his wrists. It was Rachel, and she was hurriedly cutting the bindings holding him to the post. As the creature began its crawl toward his stake, he was freed, and together, Rachel and Greg fled into the darkness.

They never spoke of that evening again. Lying awake one night, weeks later, unable to sleep for fear that the goat creature

61

would come out of nowhere to finish the job, Greg scrolled through social media.

He was surprised to see a post made by Tiffany. It was a picture of her, Maxwell, and the baby swaddled in a popcorn-patterned blanket. They all looked so happy. Tiffany's face, however, was covered in fine, white scars.

Cheap Meat

The price of groceries made Nina crazy. Living paycheck to paycheck, she signed up for every discount app, cash-back scheme, and clipped coupons where she could. Still, at the end of the month, she found herself stretching ramen noodles and canned beans as far as she could.

One day, Nina saw a tent in the parking lot of a nearly abandoned mini mall. "50% off all cuts! Free-range, no antibiotics ever!" She scanned the name of the company, CutRite Meats, and found that there were hundreds of five-star reviews online. Nina couldn't resist at least taking a look.

Once inside the tent, Nina found all types of beef and pork neatly shrink wrapped on Styrofoam trays. The meat looked fresh, and the prices were unbelievable. The man behind a short table at the far end of the tent, called her over, and told her he would give her a first-time customer discount, she just had to tell her friends. She asked why the meat was so cheap, and the man simply said, "Wholesale."

Nina piled up the steaks and chops and hurried home. She prepared one of the steaks that evening, and as the meat sizzled in the pan, the aroma filled her apartment. Her first bite tasted like heaven. Tender, juicy, and flavorful.

Nina ate her way though her haul of meats, savoring every meal. The more she ate, the more she craved the delicious taste.

She found herself eating the meat for every meal, addicted to the taste. Even her friends noticed her new obsession, especially after she tried to convince them to go to the meat tent.

"You're really into this meat, huh?" her friend Claire asked. "Where did you get it from again?"

"CutRite Meats. I swear Claire, it's the best meat I've ever tried. You should get some," Nina gushed, giddy with excitement.

After a few days, things started to get strange. Nina woke up one day with a pounding headache and a metallic taste in her mouth. It wouldn't go away regardless of how much water she drank. Her stomach growled, as though she hadn't eaten in days. She rushed to the kitchen and cooked up the few scraps of steak she had left over, gobbling them down even though they were so hot they burned her throat.

Her hunger subsided and was replaced by euphoria. She felt warm and calm, but as she glanced down, she realized her hands were stained red. At first she felt horror, but a part of her, the deep, primal part, enjoyed the sight. She washed up and ignored the incident, convinced it was an episode of low blood sugar.

Over the next few days, things only got worse for Nina. Her hunger became insatiable. Nina ate two or three steaks a meal, and her supply was dwindling. She stopped at the tent two or three times a week.

Nina even found herself in the bathroom stall at work, sneaking raw strips of beef from a zip-top sandwich bag she kept in her purse. Her headaches grew worse, and she somehow felt that her teeth were getting sharper. One look in the mirror showed that her skin was paler than usual. Her friends asked if she was feeling okay, but she dismissed them.

One day, she went to the meat tent and loaded up on more fresh steak. As she was leaving, a strange woman came out from behind a parked car and grabbed her arm.

"You need to stop this!" The woman whispered, glancing nervously toward the tent. "You need to stop eating that meat."

"Why? What are you saying?" Nina asked, irritation rising within her.

"They take people," the woman said. "People that aren't missed. Homeless, loners, drifters. That's where the meat comes from. You're eating people!"

Nina pushed the woman away, her heart pounding. "Crazy old bat," she muttered, but a cold sweat broke out across her skin. When she returned home, she looked up CutRite Meats again on her computer. Gone were the glowing, five-star reviews. In fact, she could not find CutRite Meats listed online anywhere.

A deep dread settled in. Nina raced to the refrigerator and tore open one of her remaining packages, a pack of pork chops. She looked at the meat closely. There, just on the edge where the skin would have been, was the nearly imperceptible ink outline of a dolphin. The remnants of a tattoo.

The room spun as Nina lost her balance. She crashed to the floor, but simultaneously was overcome by a gnawing hunger. Her mind splintered, caught between revulsion and craving. She tried to vomit, but nothing came up. Her mind and stomach ached, demanding to be fed.

As she knelt, curled into a ball on the floor, she felt her teeth ache and tear at her lips, becoming sharper. She held up her hands and saw her nail extend, thickening into claws. Her skin pulled tight and stretched over her creaking bones, and her consciousness slipped, replaced by the insatiable hunger for the cursed meat she had been eating.

Suddenly, there was a knock at the door. She staggered to the door, her claws now clinking on the tile. With one narrow, yellow eye, she peered through the peephole. It was her friend, Claire, looking concerned. "Nina, are you in there? You haven't been answering your phone."

Nina's mouth watered. She drew back her bleeding lips, her sharp teeth scraping together. She hesitated for a moment, trying to remember who she was and what was wrong, but the hunger thundered in her mind louder than anything else.

As she reached for the doorknob, she knew she wasn't going to let Claire leave. Not without inviting her in for dinner.

The Guest Book

Vanessa and Mark decided they needed to get away for a while. They both had stressful jobs and Vanessa thought that a weekend in a relaxed beach town was just what was needed. She decided to surprise Mark, so she went online late one night after he went to bed and found a vacation-rentals-by-owner site specific to a small beach town on the east coast.

Many of the rentals were booked by now, but she happened upon a charming baby-blue cottage right on the shore. The price was also very attractive, though it did not have many reviews. Vanessa booked the cottage, and when she told Mark, he was very excited. They packed and left the next evening.

When they arrived, the place looked immaculate. It was right on the shore, and a small wooden boardwalk led straight to the water. The sand stretched for miles in all directions, and the sound of the surf murmured pleasantly in the background.

Mark unpacked their luggage as Vanessa checked out the place. On the kitchen island was a spiral-bound book. Vanessa picked it up and saw that it was the cottage's guest book. She thumbed through a couple of the pages and smiled to herself, as guests recounted their favorite memories of their stay. Mark crashed through the door, overloaded, so she dropped the book on the counter and went to help.

Their first night was very relaxing, and they split a bottle of wine at sunset, on a blanket spread out on the beach. As the couple lay in bed, drifting off to sleep, Vanessa listened to the surf. It almost sounded like breathing.

The following day, the couple headed out to explore the town, but Vanessa couldn't find her sunglasses. Odd, she thought, as she was sure she set them down on the kitchen table. Mark couldn't find a book he had been reading. They shrugged it off and headed into town.

They decided to have a campfire the second night, using a small pit on the back deck. As the fire crackled, Mark looked up to see what he thought was a pair of eyes peering out of the kitchen window. He jumped up and yelled, "I think someone's in there!"

The two raced inside and flipped on all the lights but didn't find anyone. Mark said, "I'm starting to freak myself out a little, maybe I'm just imagining things." Vanessa picked up the discarded guest book.

She began flipping pages, and she noticed something as she got further into the entries. Guests mentioned strange noises, feelings of being watched, and more recently, a shadowy figure near the property. Some of the entries appeared frantically written, warning future guests to leave immediately.

Vanessa and Mark became more concerned but decided that it was an old cottage and people got creeped out easily. They

73

decided, because of how late it was and how they had each drank more than they were willing to drive with, that they would leave first thing in the morning.

Mark slept fitfully, and Vanessa tossed and turned. The king-sized bed felt less inviting than the first night. Mark turned over and put his arm across Vanessa, trying to get comfortable and ease his tension. A cold sweat broke out over his skin when he felt his arm slide across the sleeve of a leather jacket.

Mark slowly reached over and flipped on the bed-side lamp. He saw an older, bearded face, staring back at him. The man grinned and said, "Did you sign the guest book?"

The App

Between work and keeping up his property, Jimmy didn't have much time for social media. Further, he liked to spend his time outside, kayaking or just mowing the lawn. He had a few accounts but didn't check them regularly. He didn't use electronics to keep in touch with friends, and as a result he rarely spoke with those he did not encounter through work or through a couple outdoor clubs to which he belonged.

Jimmy met up with a couple friends for dinner one evening after work, and his friends mentioned seeing some funny videos on a new app called Wastr. "Jimmy, you gotta get Wastr. It has these videos that are unbelievable. You can even use built-in

Artificial Intelligent software to change the videos however you want. Some of these are hilarious!" his friend Seth said.

Jimmy wasn't that interested, he did like to watch some funny cat videos here and there, but his friends seemed to be enamored with the slapstick humor that the amateur-looking videos served up. He spent the remainder of the dinner nursing a beer while his friends laughed and passed around their phones with the videos blaring crazy sound effects.

Jimmy was at work a few days later, and he noticed in the lunchroom that no one was talking. Instead, they all sat in the dimly lit space staring at their little screens. "What's up?" he prodded, only to find no answer. He made his way to the microwave to heat up a pocket sandwich and noticed the bright purple Wastr app in the corner of a co-worker's screen.

Jimmy was seeing a girl he met from a hiking club, Heather, and he called her that evening to make weekend plans. She sounded distracted on their call, and when he recommended they do an overnight hike, she barely acknowledged him. After a little prodding, she admitted that she was watching some videos on Wastr, and then she spent the rest of the call in silence.

Jimmy went on the hike alone that weekend. When he returned to work the following Monday, he noticed that people all were carrying the same type of water bottle. He asked someone about it, and they said they heard about it on Wastr, and it was supposed to keep your drinks colder than any other bottle on the market.

The next day, on the television news, he overheard that the mayor was being fired by the city council after a video surfaced of him juggling ducks on Wastr. The official statement released by the city council indicated that they could not in good conscience continue to employ someone who abuses animals. The mayor's office issued a brief rebuttal denying the legitimacy of the video.

During lunch, he again went to the breakroom to heat up some food, only to see people huddled in the darkness staring at their phones, not even blinking. One staff member, stated, "This video is so bleebo."

"Yeah, super bleebo," another absently replied. Jimmy wasn't sure if bleebo was good or bad in this instance but wasn't so sure he cared. He looked around at the unmoving, unblinking masses, and shrugged his shoulders. He didn't even try to strike up a conversation this time.

A day or two later, Jimmy met up with his kayak club at the local park. When he arrived, he approached the group of kayakers gearing up to paddle. As he got closer, he realized they all carried the same water bottles as before, but now they all had red, greasy stains around their mouth. He asked one of the women about it, and she said blankly, "Everyone knows that drinking pepperoni water is good for your liver enzymes. I can't believe you didn't know." The rest of the group murmured in assent.

Pepperoni water? Jimmy thought. Things were getting very weird. As the group headed to the shore, one of them said, "Did you hear the country of Islandibadia is going to invade Novicia? That's so bleebo of the Islandibadians."

"Yeah. Bleebo deebo do," another replied.

"Super bleebo do," said another.

"Are those even real places?" Jimmy asked.

"Are you serious, Jimmy? Of course they are, why don't you look up a map on Wastr or see the videos coming out of Novicia? This is seriously bleebo deebo debie do, man," a kayaker replied. Jimmy was sure if he should laugh or scream, looking at the wild-eyed man speaking jibberish with a big greasy pepperoni stain around his mouth. He just nodded.

"Okay, man, if you say so," Jimmy replied, and kept silent the rest of the night.

Jimmy tried calling Heather again, but when she answered, she just spoke angrily about the mayor's duck scandal, the endless wars overseas, and various other topics she was enraged about. She asked if he had heard how the aliens had built a plastic shell around the planet to keep people from leaving, and that is why the sky was blue. She was worried because she didn't think they were teaching these kinds of things in school and remarked at how much else "they" were keeping from everyone. She whispered something about lemonade not being made from real lemons. As the conversation continued, Heather's words ran together until she began mumbling something that sounded like bleebo-deebo-double-dooble. Jimmy tried to cut in to end the call, stating he was tired. "Make sure you drink your pepperoni water," she sang, and hung up.

Before he knew it, Jimmy couldn't understand anyone else around him. People all started wearing the same yellow striped shirts, doing cartwheels down the sidewalk, wearing big black sunglasses, and speaking jibberish. After a while, he couldn't find anyone to communicate with. No one showed up to the kayak club or went on hikes.

One day, Jimmy had enough. He had to get out of this place, it was like he was alone in the world. Normally he wouldn't mind, he liked solitude, but this got to be too much for him. He decided he needed to get away for a while. He walked into the airport to buy a flight.

"One ticket to Islandibadia, please," he inquired.

"Bleebo deebo do," the attendant answered, with a greasy red smile. She handed him a ticket.

Remote Work

Kiera hated the morning commute. Stuck once again in traffic, she let out a string of curses and pounded the steering wheel. She realized she was sweating; her car air conditioner having given out earlier that summer. She loved her job, but the hour and a half ride was killing her, not to mention her car.

At the office, her boss yelled at her for being late, and she spilled coffee trying to catch the door to the elevator. Later that day, she was stuck contributing fifteen bucks to a baby shower for someone she never met who worked on a different floor and sat through an awkward rendition of happy birthday for one of the file clerks.

Kiera chopped away at her keyboard that afternoon after sitting through several back-to-back video meetings. As she skimmed through her email list, she noticed an unread message from a few days ago that she must have missed. The header said: JOB POSTING – REMOTE WORK.

She read through the description. Flexible work, competitive pay, work at your own pace. The job was similar to the title she currently held, but the pay was slightly more than she made now, and there was a thousand-dollar sign-on bonus. She liked the idea of working from home, but wondered if she would be lonely. She ignored it and moved on to other things.

Kiera noticed a week or so later that several offices near hers were empty. She asked her boss, and she told Kiera that several employees were leaving for some new remote work opportunity. Kiera's boss said their company couldn't compete with the terms, and their corporate office wasn't interested in allowing employees to work remotely.

Kiera noticed one of the empty offices belonged to her friend Stephen, so she called him later that day. He confirmed that he had received a similar email and when he contacted the company, they were eager to onboard him immediately, and offered him double the sign-on bonus if he started that week. "Yeah, I just started a couple days ago but so far it seems really cool. I've only started on a project, but it seems pretty straightforward. Hey, if you sign on, we both get an extra five hundred," he said.

Kiera decided to contact the company, and after a few calls and a video conference with a very pleasant recruiter, she was signed up and ready to go. The recruiter said they would be shipping her a company laptop express, and when it arrived, she could get started with the orientation process. Kiera put in her notice at her old job immediately.

The laptop arrived as promised, a generous-sized system with an 18-inch screen. Her recruitment bonus hit her account the next day. Kiera set up a workstation at her kitchen bar and planned to commence the next day.

Kiera's first few days were uneventful, logging in dutifully and hitting the big red button on the top right-hand corner of the keyboard that the company required when an employee started their work hours. Kiera was recommended to log a minimum of 40 hours throughout the week, but unless she was scheduled for meetings or sales calls, she could complete those at any time of the day or night. The hours had to be completed between midnight on Monday and 11:59pm on the following Sunday.

Kiera found that she liked working throughout the day, logging in for an hour or two, taking a break to do housework or take a walk. She felt unfettered, free of a bothersome commute, annoying co-workers, and the obligation to an eight-hour block of work.

The work was easy enough, but soon she began to get a little bored. The tasks she was assigned were initially interesting and challenging, but after a couple of weeks, they seemed somewhat repetitive. She was asked to compile endless seemingly similar presentations, write goal and objective lists to send to her supervisors, and log random numbers in spreadsheets.

Within a month, Kiera found she could complete her assigned tasks in far fewer hours than the 40, and she figured since she was so efficient, she stopped keeping track. She was salary, anyway.

One day around two o'clock in the afternoon, she was sitting on her couch reading a book when a loud siren went off on her computer. She rushed over and clicked the red button to log on, only to be confronted with a stern-looking man.

"You have only logged 23 hours this week, Kiera. You'll be docked pay next time you fall below 40 hours," the man said tersely, then ended the conference. Kiera began to panic, realizing she had been slacking.

Several times over the next work week, Kiera was alerted by the loud siren at odd hours. Sometimes, she was told she had not logged enough hours in a session, so she was forced to log in and put in more time. Other times, if she was at her work station, the siren was accompanied by a text box telling her to take a break.

Soon, she received an email from corporate, informing her of a new wellness program. It would periodically interrupt her work

87

session if she had been sitting too long and reminded her to get up and move around. If she complied with this wellness program, she would earn an additional hundred dollars per week as a stipend. The email stated that studies found a reduction in health care premiums for active employees.

Keira would find herself interrupted from tasks to stretch, do yoga, or dance. Sometimes, the workstation would play upbeat music, and a bouncing ball would appear on screen. She was asked to march in place, and the ball bounced up and down based on how fast she marched.

If Kiera missed the prompt, or if she didn't perform the task as stated, the laptop would buzz at her, the activity time would end, and the siren would play, directing her to return to her workstation.

Kiera didn't enjoy this part of her new job, but sure enough the stipend appeared in her weekly check. As annoying as the interruptions were, she admitted it added some variety to an otherwise endless series of menial tasks. Further, she still felt like she had a lot of flexibility in her life, and the job was extremely easy.

At the grocery store one day, Kiera felt like a woman was staring at her. She dismissed the feeling, as she was not getting out of the house as much as she liked, on account of the odd work hours she was keeping. However, she couldn't shake the feeling as every aisle she went down, she felt the eyes of other customers. She left the store and noticed the same thing walking down the street. Then, near an outdoor restaurant, a small child pointed at her and said, "Look mommy! It's her!"

Kiera hurried back to her apartment, her heart racing. Why was everyone noticing her? Her phone buzzed, and it was her mother. She breathlessly commanded that Kiera turn on the television to channel 10. Kiera did so and was shocked. She watched herself falling during a yoga pose, then a quick cut to her marching in place in her bathrobe. The clip flashed to an unflattering upward angle of her face as she flossed her teeth, and another of her doing a silly dance.

"Don't miss tonight's episode of *Watch'em Work,* where these employees work for *you!*" the announcer shouted. Kiera stood there speechless. She pulled out her phone and quickly searched *Watch'em Work,* and found still images of her, some of her former coworkers, and other strangers, all milling about their homes and caught in awkward dance poses. She navigated to the show's homepage.

The page described the show as an interactive reality experience, where an audience tuned in to a livestream of a real employee, and the audience could spend money to vote on tasks for the employees to perform. The highlight reel featured Kiera's commercial clips.

She ran over to her workstation, which had begun blaring the siren she had become all too familiar with. She closed the laptop, threw it in the trash, and ran out of her apartment.

Two days later, Kiera, called a lawyer and after some research, learned that she had signed an agreement form when

she accepted the job, which she obviously had not read. She returned to her job and sheepishly asked to be re-hired, only to be told she didn't seem like a good fit for the company.

That night, defeated, she sat on the couch and turned on the TV. It was another episode of *Watch'em Work*. There, other unsuspecting folks jumped and stretched, oblivious they had an audience. Kiera's blood ran cold when at the end of the segment, a video played of her sleeping in bed. Her workstation was never in her bedroom.

The Travel Team

Becky's son Aiden was an excellent football player. He started as soon as he was able to join the Pee Wee league and was now entering his second year in the competitive junior league. He loved the game, and every minute he was not at school or doing homework, he watched football, practiced throwing and catching, and studied the game.

Aiden was very good for his age, and during many games, he was a standout amongst the confused, clumsy players around him. He was even picked by the coach to start most games as the quarterback, and his junior league team was winning the regular season this year.

Becky was sitting in the bleachers one autumn afternoon when she was approached by a man wearing a satin sports jacket. "Your son is really good," he started, "but he isn't going to get the play time he needs to stand out unless he gets involved in something more competitive."

"I'm not sure, he seems to be having fun here," Becky replied.

"Well, if you're thinking about his future, I'd consider travel," the man said. He gave her a flyer for a team, and introduced himself as Bud Billings, the coach for the travel team. He told her he would guarantee him more playing time than he was currently getting.

"It depends on what kind of future you see for Aiden, if he's here for the love of the game, that's fine, but if he's competitive, there's only one way to go," Bud admonished. Becky didn't know if she saw herself as a sports mom. She had a busy social life and loved her job, but it required extra hours every week. Still, she didn't want to rob her son of an opportunity. She decided to talk to him about it after the game.

When Becky showed Aiden the crumpled flyer, he jumped around with excitement. He said that some other kids were thinking of joining a travel team, but when they tried out, they weren't good enough. He begged his mom to call Coach Billings and get him a try-out.

Becky took Aiden later that week down to a ball field at a closed-down public school. Coach Billings and a few other men met them there, and they ran Aiden through a series of drills, testing his capabilities. Then, they shoved a stack of papers at Becky. She thumbed through them, but they were pages of team rules, codes of conduct, statements of commitment, and of course, the registration fee.

Becky gulped when she saw that the registration fee was as much as a few months' rent in a nice apartment. She also scanned and saw that travel required a minimum number of games and practices to be attended. She envisioned her social life going up in smoke. Still, she didn't want to rob her son of an opportunity.

After the tryout, Coach Billings said, "Well, what'll it be?"

"Can we think it over?" Becky replied. Aiden glared up at her.

"What's there to think about, mom?" He whispered. Becky panicked and signed the last page.

"Do you take checks?" She said, pulling out her checkbook and dating the check two days into the future, payday. Coach Billings grinned back and told her they wouldn't regret it. Aiden was going to the big time. He also said that practice started Saturday, and their first game would be in two weeks. Becky gulped again, but she didn't want to rob her son of an opportunity.

Practice started, and it was five days a week, with at least one game a week. Becky quickly settled into a routine of driving to practice, which was 40 minutes away from home, where she sat in the car and waited for Aiden to be done. At first she didn't mind, but practices grew longer and longer, and before she knew it, she was getting home at one or two in the morning. Aiden, however, did not seem bothered, and was as happy and enthusiastic as ever.

Then the games started. Becky was driving all over the northeast on the weekends. She stopped hearing from her friends and didn't find that she fit in well with the other sports parents. The games were long, the travel longer, and soon tournaments started. She had to cut back hours at work, which caused her to get passed up for a promotion. Still, she didn't want to rob her son of an opportunity.

Coach Billings tapped Becky on the shoulder after one game, waking her from a sound sleep. He told her that there was actually one more game to play after this and gave her directions for the two games tomorrow. He also pulled out the last page of the commitment she had signed, and at the bottom was small print that informed her the registration fee was actually only the first installment of an annual plan. Becky sighed, dug out her checkbook, and dated it for a week into the future, payday. She didn't want to rob her son of an opportunity.

Years went by, and people still speak of a woman named Becky, clad in black leggings and an oversized hoodie, sleeping on the top of the bleachers in some town down the highway. As the story goes, she doesn't have a house anymore, and lives out of her SUV. She's never in the same place for too long, her voice is hoarse from yelling, and her wallet's empty. Still, she didn't want to rob her son of an opportunity.

99

J.R. Salem

Dear Recipient,

We hope you've enjoyed your time with Scary Stories to Tell Millennials. Your feedback is incredibly valuable to us, and we'd love to hear about your experience. If you found the book enjoyable, fun, or just what you needed, would you consider leaving a review on Amazon?

Your review helps others discover the book and lets us know what we're doing right—or where we can improve. Plus, it's a great way to support our work and ensure that we can continue creating products that bring a bit of joy and stress relief to the world. Thank you so much for your support!

Warm regards,

J. R. Salem

J. R. SALEM

Made in the USA
Monee, IL
07 October 2024